# Table of Contents

| Subject Matter | Pages |
|---|---|
| **Lesson 1: Leading vs. Managing** | 4-14 |
|     Qualities of Leadership | |
|     Ethical Leadership | |
|     Understanding the Culture | |
|     Becoming a Moral Leader | |
| **Lesson 2: Learn to Listen** | 15-17 |
| **Lesson 3: Managing Change** | 18-20 |
| **Lesson 4: Measuring Outcomes and Performance** | 21-27 |
|     *Formulas:* | |
|     Cost Per Hire | |
|     Interviewing Costs | |
|     Quality of Hire | |
|     Employee Suggest for Improvement | |
|     Earned Value Analysis for | |
|         Project Management | |
|         Estimation of Completion | |
| **Lesson 5: Communicating Outcomes** | 28-35 |
|     *Diagrams:* | |
|     Affinity Diagram | |
|     Interrelationship Diagraphs | |
|     Tree Diagram | |
|     Matrix Diagram | |
|     Matrix Data Analysis | |
|     Process Decision Program Chart | |
|     Arrow Diagrams | |
| Future Book Topics | 36 |
| References | 37 |
| Appendix A: Article | 38 |
| Appendix B: Exercise on Ethics | 39 |
| Appendix C: Listening Exercises | 40-45 |
| Appendix D: Cameron Clue – Cameron's Change Model | 46 |
| Appendix E: Cameron Clue – Writing the Business Proposal | 47 |
| Appendix F: Cameron Clue – Communication Plan | 48-49 |
|     Author Information | 50 |

# 5 Lessons the Board Member Needs to Know

The HOA Board of Directors (BOD) and the Community Managers today are expected to be specialists. Therefore, both the BOD and the Community Management Company need to be stable, organized and have the ability to clearly understand the strengths, weaknesses, opportunities and threats (SWOT Analysis) within the community, homeowners and elected board officers. An excellent business tool to assist is the SWOT analysis, which can be developed to assist the HOA in leading and managing the community.

The SWOT example below focuses on the HOA and includes analyzing the HOA's "strengths" of competency, financial structure, expertise of board and/or management to name a few. At the same time noting any "weaknesses" in those areas and researching the external factors that may jeopardize the community. Some external "opportunities" that will set your HOA apart from others is the ability to offer diversified related services. Today permanent HOA residents both young and seniors are looking for communities that keep them connected, thereby allowing them the opportunity to socialize. Vacation properties with HOA's are also seeing an increase in visitors requesting social activities and services for children. Another important factor to consider from external competition is market growth in the way of maintaining property values, which includes managing reserves. When the HOA gives attention to addressing the changing needs of the homeowners the community will note that as an opportunity over competition within the analysis report. HOA's that do not keep up to these standards than they are listed as "threats" and not opportunities.

# HOA SWOT Analysis

| INTERNAL ||
|---|---|
| **Strengths** | **Weaknesses** |
| A distinctive competence | No clear strategic direction |
| Adequate financial resources | A deteriorating competitive position |
| Good contacts/relations with homeowners | Lack of managerial depth and talent |
| Good Competitive Skills | Missing any key skills or competencies |
| Special expertise | Poor track record in implementing strategy |
| Well-conceived functional area strategies | Plagued with internal operating problems |
| Innovative Programs/Services | Vulnerable to competitive pressures |
| Good overall reputation | Too narrow a service line |
| Access to economies of scale | Weak market image |
| Insulated from strong competitive pressure | Competitive disadvantages |
| Cost advantages | Below-average marketing skills |
| Competitive advantages | Unable to finance needed changes in strategy |
| Proven management | Other??? |

| EXTERNAL ||
|---|---|
| **Opportunities** | **Threats** |
| Diversify into related services | Slow market growth |
| Complacency among rival HOA | Growing competitive pressures |
| Fast market growth | Vulnerability to recession and business cycle |
| Weak competitors | Changing of homeowner needs and tastes |
| Lack of dominant competitor | Adverse demographic changes |
| Other??? | Other??? |

Therefore, the lessons in book TWO will review topics to assist leaders and managers within the HOA community in making decisions and solving problems. Lessons on listening, measuring outcomes and reporting the findings are included. After all a good leader must be a good listener in order to recognize and evaluate problems, measure performance, and communicate and implement the changes necessary for success. In performing all these duties the **HOA Board** will **LEAD** and the **Community Manager** will **MANAGE**.

# LESSON 1: Leading Vs. Managing

The focus of this lesson will be on the Homeowners Associations (HOA) Board of Directors (BOD) ability to separate the duties and responsibilities of **Leading vs. Managing,** and to further understand the skills-set and foundational knowledge each function requires. With the most common failures of an HOA or Community Manager being that of having an over-managed or under-led community we begin this booklet by providing instructions on how to do "the balancing act."

## Leading

The role of the **HOA BOD leaders** is to produce major change, often large and dramatic change for the purpose of the community to survive and prosper. The vision of leading is to improve the community so that it continues to be a viable investment, and secure and safe environment for homeowners. When each Board member understands his/her responsibilities, as well as, the roles of the property management company, the HOA Board will operate more effectively and efficiently. The BOD's **strategy as leaders** are to develop community wide strategic objectives to improve and remain competitive.

- Quickly diagnose problems
- Quickly correct the situation
- Sustain gains
- Become goal oriented

## Managing

The **Community Management Company's** role is that of **managing** the community by designing procedures and processes that create predictable and orderly outcomes, such as: excellent communication, good quality service, being on budget, to name a few. Excellent management is conservative, methodically incremental and short-term oriented. Communities have different administrative needs, so management companies offer a wide range of services that should be outlined in the contract. The Management Company's **strategy as managers** is to implement action plans to achieve the strategic objectives designed by the BOD's.

- Clear understanding of what is happening with finances
- System and procedurally oriented

This **foundation of knowledge** begins by reviewing the skills required to manage and lead. In John Kotter's book, *A Force for Change* (Free Press 1990), he describes the distinction between management and leadership as illustrated in the table below. He states that both management and leadership, uses different techniques.

## Comparison of Management and Leadership Skills

| Needs | Management Skills | Leadership Skills |
|---|---|---|
| Creating an agenda | Planning and budgeting | Establishing a vision for the future and the strategies to produce the changes needed |
| Developing a human network to accomplish the agenda | Organizing and staff | Aligning people though communication and deeds so the change occurs with horizontal and vertical integration |
| Execution of the agenda | Controlling and problem solving | Motivating and inspiring so everyone can contribute to changing the entire system |

In an HOA both the Board of Directors and the Management Company must WORK TOGETHER and LEAD the community! Therefore, this lesson will focus on Leadership and the competencies, characteristics, perspective and performance required from both the **HOA Board** in **LEADING** and the **Community Manager** in **MANAGING**.

## History of Leadership

We begin with Psychologist Kurt Lewin who in 1939 identified three different styles of leadership. In his early study he classified the <u>autocratic leaders</u> who provided clear expectations for what needed to be done, when and how focusing on both command by the leader and control.

The second style is <u>participative leadership</u> also known as democratic leadership that guides its members and accepts their input. This style was found to be the most productive. The last style Lewin identified was known as <u>laissez-faire leadership</u> and it was the least productive of all three styles. These members made more demands on the leader, showed little cooperation and were unable to work independently.

Throughout the years many different leadership theories/styles have emerged to explain how and why certain people become great leaders. Here eight management theories are listed in the table below for I support the opinion that Leadership continues to lean on each of them. The Great Man theory from the 1840's where people believed leaders are born with the ability to lead. Through the 1950's Behavioral theories that were based on the belief that leaders are made. Right up to theories of the 1970's where Relational theories focused on the relationship and connection the leaders have with followers.

Therefore, I believe that all the theories of our yester years exist in forming the leaders today and these historical theories will continue to form the leaders of tomorrow.

"According to your résumé, you were an Egyptian Pharaoh in a past life. Have you updated your leadership skills since then?"

> **Interesting Article titled**
> *Are you Confusing Leadership with Control?*
> **Can be found in Appendix A**

| 8 Major Leadership Theories |||
|---|---|---|
| **Theory** | **Year** | **Characteristics** |
| **Great Man Theories** | 1840's | People are born with the ability to lead. They have charisma, confidence, intelligence and social skills - the natural born leader! |
| **Trait Theories** | 1930-1940's | People inherit certain qualities and traits that make them suited to leadership. Earliest work was from Carl Jung's theory named Myers and Briggs personality test. |
| **Contingency Theories** | Mid 1960's | Particular variables related to the environment determines which style of leadership is best for the situation. Fiedler's Contingency Model. |
| **Situational Theories** | Mid 1970's | Like Contingency this theory has the leader selecting the best course of action based upon the situation. Work of Hersey and Blanchard Life Cycle Theory of Leadership. |
| **Behavioral Theories** | 1940-1950's | Based upon a belief that great leaders are made, not born and it is rooted in behaviorism and that one can learn leadership. |
| **Participative Theories (MBO –Management by Objectives)** | 1960's | Suggest that the ideal leadership style is one that take the input of others into account. Participation and contributions are encouraged. |
| **Management Theories (Transactional theory)** | 1970's | Focuses on the role of supervision, rewards and accountability of ones actions. |
| **Relationship Theories (Transformational theory)** | 1970's | Focuses on the relationship and connection the leader has with followers. Motivation and inspiration are seen as important factors. |

## Qualities of Leadership for the HOA

Leadership is the ability to positively influence the homeowners and systems under the authority of the Board of Directors to have a meaningful impact and achieve important results. This is accomplished through clear and visible values and integrating those values into the Associations strategy and structure. Leaders should be good role models, knowledgeable about HOA local, state and federal laws and certainly the governing documents for the community. However, today the HOA leaders must understand much more with the most important ability being an expertise in current Business practices and ethical leadership theories. Aligning the ethical leadership and community culture with total quality management, and "lean and mean" concepts are required to bring the community into the 21st Century. Therefore, the following qualities of leadership should be identified when interviewing and voting for the leaders within your HOA community.

### 9 Qualities of Leadership for the HOA

| 9 Qualities of Leadership for the HOA ||
|---|---|
| Quality | Explanation |
| **Competencies** | Navigator, Communicator, Mentor, Learner, Builder and Motivator. |
| **Personal Leadership Characteristics** | Accountability, Courage, Humility, Integrity, Creativity, Perseverance and Well-being. |
| **Strategic Leadership** | Requires ability to create a viable future for the community and to gain a competitive advantage. Ability to: Anticipate, Maintain flexibility, think strategically and work with others to initiate changes. |
| **Activities of Strategic Leadership** | Activities of creating and communicating a vision of the future, sustaining an effective organization culture, making strategic decisions, developing key competencies and responsibilities, managing multiple constituencies, and instilling ethical value systems into the communities culture. |
| **Capabilities** | Absorptive capacity (the ability for a community to learn) Adaptive capacity (the ability of a community to change) |
| **Leadership System** | Leadership is exercised, formally and informally, throughout a community. Elements include: how key decisions are made and communicated, and how decisions are carried out at all levels. Includes structures and mechanisms for: decision making, selection and development of leaders and managers, reinforcement of values and performance expectations. |
| **Leadership Theories** | Understand the differences in leadership styles and contexts to help provide guidance to the BOD in pursuing performance excellence, and when to apply each one. They include: Situational leadership, Transactional leadership theory, Transformational leadership theory, Substitutes for leadership theory, and Emotional intelligence theory. |
| **Governance & Social Responsibility** | Corporate Social responsibility (CSR) relates to responsibility to the public through the practices of good citizenship and includes ethics, aspects of corporate governance, and protection of public health, safety, and the environment. Corporate social responsibility has become a strategic imperative and a competitive or marketplace necessity. **Governance processes may include:** Approving strategic direction, Monitoring and evaluating CEO performance, Succession planning, Financial auditing, Executive compensation, and Disclosure Shareholder reporting. |
| **Commitment** | Critical to success! **It requires:** Aligning objectives with the goals of BOD and homeowners, using quantitative arguments, developing sympathetic allies and getting early "wins." |

# Ethical Leadership

Ethics is the beliefs about what is right and wrong and good and bad. These beliefs are based on both individual beliefs and social concepts. Ethical practices vary from person to person, business to business and culture to culture; however, general ethical principles do exist.

## Ethical Principles
1. Do unto others, as you would have them do unto you – The Golden Rule
2. If an action is not right for everyone to take, then it is not right for anyone – Immanuel Kant's Categorical Imperative
3. If an action cannot be taken repeatedly, then it is not right to take at all – Descartes' rule of change
4. Take the action that achieves the higher or greater value – The Unitarian Principle
5. Take the action that produces the least harm, or incurs the least potential cost – Risk Aversion Principle

**Ethical behavior –** The way the BOD, homeowner or community manager conforms to generally acceptable social norms about what is right and good.

Unethical behavior – social norms of what is wrong and bad

**Business Ethics –** is a term often used to refer to ethical or unethical behaviors by the BOD, homeowner or community manager when operating within an HOA.

## HOA's steps to Ethical Practices:

- **Ethical Analysis**
1. Identify and describe clearly the facts
2. Define the conflict or dilemma and identify the higher-order values involved
3. Identify the stakeholders (Employees, Homeowners, Vendors)
4. Identify the options that you can reasonably take
5. Identify the potential consequences of your options

- **Written codes – CODE OF CONDUCT** that include:
    a. values & principles used to guide decisions
    b. effective training of expectations
    c. measure of accomplishments
    d. outcome report

- **Ethics Programs and Orientations –** to inform homeowners/employees of the ethical policy, training required, measuring, and outcomes to expect

- **Dimensions of the Information Age**

*1. Information Rights: Privacy and Freedom in the Internet Age*

Most American and European privacy law is based on the Fair Information Practices (FIP) written in 1973 by a federal government advisory committee.

**Those principles are:**
- There should be no personal record systems whose existence is secret
- Individuals have rights of access, inspection, review, and amendment to systems that contain information about them
- There must be no use of personal information for purposes other than those for which it was gathered without prior consent.
- Managers of systems are responsible and can be held accountable and liable for the damage done by systems for their reliability and security.
- Governments have the right to intervene in the information relationships among private parties.

The Privacy Act of 1974 expanded from these principles and is the most important law that regulated the federal government's collection, use, and disclosure of information.

*2. Property Rights: Intellectual Property*

Trade Secrets, Copyright, and Patents to protect Intellectual Property.

*3. Accountability, Liability, and Control*

New Information technologies are challenging existing liability law and social practices for holding individuals and institutions accountable.

*4. System Quality: Data Quality and System Errors <u>and</u>*

*5. Quality of Life: Equity, Access, Boundaries*

It is written that Computers and Information technologies potentially can destroy valuable elements of our culture and society even while they bring us benefits. This is mainly due to the negative social consequences, such as:
- The decentralization of decision making to lower organizational levels, which has reduced power in organizations
- Reduced response time to competition – rapid change – can't keep up
- Boundaries are being infringed on – family – work – leisure
- Dependency on technology
- Computer Crime and Abuse
- Loss of Jobs
- Question if access to technology will close the culture and social gaps in society or increase and widen it!!!!
- Health risks – (Repetitive stress injuries) (Carpel Tunnel syndrome)

The goal for each of us is to become Ethical Leaders, therefore, answer the following questions to quickly identify if an action you are ready to undertake is truly an **Ethical Action.**

Are you consistent with the HOA's goals and not motivated by self-interest?

Does the action respect the rights of individuals?

Does the action meet the standards of fairness and equity?

Would you wish others to behave in the same way if the action affected you?

**IF you answered YES to each question than it was an Ethical Choice!**

**Another Exercise on Ethics Found in Appendix B**

# Understanding the Culture

Culture is a system of shared beliefs and values that develop within an HOA Community or group and guides the behavior of its homeowners/members. A general description of a leader might be someone who is charismatic and seeks to develop a transformational style of leadership. Charismatic/transformational leadership is thought to broaden and elevate the interests of followers, generate awareness and acceptance among the followers of the purpose and mission of the group and motivate followers to go beyond their self-interests for the good of the organization. But different cultural groups may vary in their conceptions of the most important characteristics of charismatic/transformational leadership. In some cultures, one might need to take strong, decisive action in order to be seen as a leader, while in other cultures consultation and a democratic approach may be the preferred approach to exercising effective leadership. Managerial practices and motivational techniques that are legitimate and acceptable in one culture may not be in another.

## What does it do?
1. Establishes a personality for the HOA Community
2. Influences the behaviors of the homeowners
3. Gives the public (visitors) symbols of the HOA and provides stories and history about the community

## How do we find out about the culture within the HOA Community?
1. Stories: About the life of the HOA Community
2. Heroes: Accomplishments of HOA board members or community managers within the Community
3. Rituals: Special occasions and performance ceremonies
4. Symbols: Verbal and non-verbal communication and visual themes

**Multicultural HOA Community:** Operates within a culture and is based on the following:
1. Pluralism: Minority and majority cultures work together to influence the values and policies of the community
2. Structural Integration: Minority cultures are seen in all levels and in all functions
3. Information Network Integration: Mentoring and support groups help the minority culture develop

## Becoming a Moral Leader

A Moral Leader is a very different kind of leadership. Moral Leaders are not aspired to be followed they aim to serve and develop the capacities of others. This leader is not about rank, money or status. The Moral Leader can be characterized by a deep sense of ethics and core values and are motivated by the pursuit of a higher purpose. They work to overcome obstacles and are skilled at the art of consultation and unity.

| 10 Ways to Act Like a Moral Leader |
| --- |
| 1. Uphold high moral standards |
| 2. Focus on doing what is right for the community and homeowners |
| 3. Set the example you want others to follow |
| 4. Be honest and trustworthy |
| 5. Eliminate fear and become approachable |
| 6. Establish and communicate ethical practices |
| 7. Show zero tolerance for ethical violations |
| 8. Reward ethical conduct |
| 9. Treat everyone the same…with dignity, fairness and respect |
| 10. Do the right thing at the right time for the right reasons |

When homeowners within the HOA and/or the employees of the management company say they want their voices to be heard, they really are saying they want the leaders to listen. Leaders who are excellent listeners create trustworthy relationships that are transparent and breed loyalty. Furthermore, leaders must become more mindful of homeowners needs in order to effectively inspire professional performance. This leads into our next lesson on how to become a more effective LISTENER.

# LESSON 2: Learn to LISTEN

The HOA Board member and Community Manager both need to take responsibility for gathering accurate, timely and relevant information, and the common ways to accomplish that are by developing good observation and listening skills. Part of being a good communicator means knowing how to LISTEN.

*Do you do PSEUDO LISTENING?*
*That is when you pretend to be listening!*

- People hear 20,000 to 30,000 words during the day.
- People spend 70% to 80% of the day communicating in some way.
- 55% of a person's day is spent listening to others.
- Average person says about 125 to 175 words per day.
- Average number of words you listen to per minute is about 500.
- Only 7% of your spoken message is conveyed for 93% of the message is delivered through facial expressions.
- Research shows that MEN only use half their brain to listen while WOMEN engage both lobes.

**Benefits of Good Listening**
　**For the HOA Board Member** – the ability to gather info on and gain knowledge about your homeowners and community
　**For the Community Manager** – helps obtain inside info about the community and board

**Problems with Ineffective Listening**
1. **Perceived as Less Intelligent** – perceived to NOT be able to handle what is being said, and/or can't understand what is being said.

2. **Poor Listening is Costly** – it waste time, requires repeating of messages, inaccurate project material ordering and/or costs.

3. **Poor Listening Limits your Chances for Success** – it does not portray competence; therefore, overlooked for promotions, salary increases, recognition, re-election, etc.

## PERCEPTION

**Perception** – process of creating meaning based on experiences.

1. **Factors Influencing Perception –**
   **Reception** – physical process of hearing and seeing
   **Attention** – is the cognitive ability that allows us to select certain types of information for processing and ignoring others

2. **Assessing your own Perceptions** – problems occur when false impressions distorts your interpretation.

3. **Assessing Others Perceptions –**
   **Sympathy** – identification with others feelings
   **Empathy** – the act of sharing the feelings of another person

## DISTRACTIONS

**Environmental Distractions** – noise, multi-tasking, driving, cell phones
**Emotional Distractions** – your feelings at time you are listening, if irate not listening
**Message Content** – small talk, social abilities, personal, which all have different distractions

### Become a more interactive listener by:

1. **Talking Less** - practice listening.
2. **Asking more Questions** – closed and open questions and probing.
3. **Using Nonverbal Behavior** – to comprehend what you are understanding by nodding and/or gesturing.
4. **Dismantling the Three D's –**
   **Distractions** – move the focus of attention away from the message.
   **Disorientation** – breakdown in the mental and emotion process.
   **Defensiveness** – produces biased judgment about messages because of overly emotional feelings.
5. **Fighting Boredom** – we process on average 500 words per minute, but average speech is 150 words per minute. Watch for boredom in delivery.

## ACTIVE LISTENING

**In order for LISTENING to be successful you <u>must</u> be an *active participant* in the communication process.**

The **listener is *actively*** working while the speaker is talking. This happens because our thought speed is much faster than our speech speed. <u>You have to control your thought speed, so not to let it turn into daydreaming and/or boredom.</u>

In *Active Listening* two things must take place before the LISTENER can respond to a speaker they are:
- A. Identify the meaning of the message
- B. Evaluate the message

## Eight Suggestions for Active Listening:

1. **Set a purpose for listening.** – What do you want to achieve? (Examples)
    - A. Details of the topic
    - B. Improved note taking
    - C. Better ability to participate in a discussion
    - D. Stay awake during work/meetings

2. **Concentrate on the message by eliminating internal and external distractions.**

3. **Think of questions.** Jot down questions to ask during meetings.

4. **Capitalize on your faster thought speed.** – Use this time wisely!

    Predict – What will be discussed next
    Evaluate – The evidence presented
    Find links – Places to go to find more information

5. **Listen for transitions,** which are clues to various parts of a lecture.

Introduction or Summary
- A. Today's Meeting Covers…
- B. Today I'd like to discuss…
- C. Let's look at
- D. To summarize
- E. As a review
- F. Recapping
- G. In conclusion

Compare and Contrast
- A. Similar to, both, likewise
- B. However, on the other hand, instead,

Cause and Effect
- A. The cause of, for this reason, because
- B. As a result, therefore

6. **Hear the speaker out!**
    - A. Don't jump to conclusions
    - B. Don't stop listening
    - C. Don't give up because subject is difficult

> *How well are you at Listening?*
> **Listening Exercises found in Appendix C**

7. **Be alert for other verbal and non-verbal cues.**
    - A. Changes in tone of voice
    - B. Items written on board or handouts
    - C. Specific phrases e.g., last meeting some homeowners brought up…

8. **Be prepared and be flexible.**

# LESSON 3: Managing CHANGE

　　　CHANGE is often a hierarchical process where the leaders of an organization or in this case the HOA Board of Directors decide if a policy or procedure needs to be changed. When change is necessary the leaders/HOA boards decide when and how the change would be introduced. The employees/homeowners have little input into the process, so the change is sometimes pushed and/or forced. Resistance to change is often high, and moral and motivation is often low; therefore, it is vital to success that all parties learn to manage CHANGE! Managing the acceptance of change is a challenging encounter. Change will happen for without it the community will not grow and improve. Although most change is still a hierarchical process when it comes to policy making, it is the communication and philosophy of how to introduce CHANGE, which has changed. Today communication travels rapidly within the organization/community, because of the internet, email and technology. The internet has flattened the hierarchical diagram (Disintermediation, see page 27) and has allowed employees/homeowners to send emails thereby sharing information and their opinions before leaders/board of directors have the opportunity to explain or fully justify their actions.

## Why HOA and Communities are Rapidly Changing
1. Change is More Acceptable
2. Technology is Ever Changing
3. Knowledge is expected

**The nature of work is changing.**
- Learning and speed are IN
- Habit and Complacency are OUT
- Command and control is OUT
- Information and Technology is IN
- Teams are IN
- Empowerment is IN
- Expectations of workers due to learning is more towards performance is IN

# The Traditional Change Models

Lewin's Change Model below presented early stages of change included shock and denial where one refuses to believe what is happening and instead believes everything will be all right. This is followed by guilt and anger until the acceptance and/or acknowledgement is acquired.

Lewin's Change Model in 1951 discussed 3 stages.

> Stage 1 – Un-Freezing
> > This is where the un-learning of old attitudes and behavior patterns were performed.
> 
> Stage 2 – Change
> > In this stage the change was consolidated into existing processes and procedures.
> 
> Stage 3 – Re-Freezing
> > Resistance to change was addressed and the "new attitude and behavior" was adhered to and followed.

# Cameron's Transitional Change Model

Today the change agents have to be aware of this instantaneous delivery, and although they cannot control it, they can prepare for it. Leaders/HOA boards must include their employees/homeowners in the decision making process, which can be done by forming committees. Committees permit the stakeholders to have input into change or addressing issues and this will greatly decrease the negative discussions about the change and increase the positive input. (You can find more on Committees in Book ONE of our HOA Series) Listening to your employees/homeowners will enable a decrease of the change process and an increase into moral and motivation. Therefore, Dr. Cameron designed a new change model that was first introduced into lecture in 2009 and presented here as well.

# Dr. Cameron's Formula for Implementing Change
## G + O + A + L + S = Successful Change©

| | |
|---|---|
| **G** | From the beginning the **GOALS** and need for the change must be discussed, planned, and communicated to all stakeholders that it will affect. Organize a committee that is charged with developing the change process. The committee will develop and administer a survey that will be distributed to the department or entire company. This will keep all stakeholders informed and get their input on the change process. |
| **O** | The change must be **OBTAINABLE and ORGANIZED**. The change must be needed and an obtainable change. The change must be realistic. If it is not realistic it will not be accepted and therefore, implantation will not be successful. Also the change process should be presented in an organized, well designed and communicated process to not only those affected, but to the entire company. Explain the "why, when and how" the change will be taking place. The more details the better. (*The Road to Success is Paved with Details*. A poster designed by William D. Cameron) |
| **A** | There should be an **ANNOUNCEMENT** and REWARD to those that embrace the change. Rewards can be verbal recognition, a monetary award or a gift. It should be a company-wide **announcement** and be well communicated. This will foster future cooperation in implementing change within your organization. |
| **L** | After the change is implemented make sure you **LISTEN** to your employees. Address resistance to the change by again reminding the employee of the "why" the change was necessary. Also make sure supervisors are addressing any negative talk happening within the company, and do not ignore it. |
| **S** | **SHARE** feedback. Make sure the **SUCCESSES** and failures of the change implementation are noted, recorded and discussed. This will ensure future successful change! |

After effective listening and understanding how to handle change the Board and/or Community Manager should be aware of issues that need to be addressed and how to introduce them to their homeowners. An Analysis and **Measuring of Performance** that was identified through facts and data will provide a basis for effective decision making within the community. Furthermore, it will provide the HOA with a foundation for the Board and Community Management Company to review and assess how well strategic objectives and action plans are progressing.

**Cameron Clue on the Change Model can be found in Appendix D**

# LESSON 4: Measuring Outcomes & Performance

The goal of every HOA Board, and Community Management Company is to lead and manage so that the organization operates efficiently, effectively and maintains a customer oriented environment. Therefore, measuring outcomes and performance is vital to the success of the HOA and an important lesson to learn. Measures should include a combination of strategic and operational measures to identify the impact on the homeowners and the community at large. An outdated measurement system wastes resources, hinders strategic deployment, and often rewards wrong behaviors. Therefore, an annual audit of the measurement system should be conducted to confirm that the HOA's goals are aligned with the measures, and that the right balance between leading measures (performance drivers) and lagging measures (outcomes) exist between operational and strategic plans. Understand that <u>everything is measurable</u> and in order to evaluate cost reductions and/or cost avoidance activities measuring needs to take place.

**Costs Reduction** - *increased productivity allows fewer employees to do more in less time*
**Cost Increase** – *new equipment*
**Cost Avoidance** – *staff not needed*

Effective performance measures and indicators used by the HOA's Board of Directors should be aligned with business strategy and should be driven by internal and external factors that shape the Associations operating environment.

**Linking Measures to the HOA Strategy will:**
- Lead to actions incongruent with strategies, even if they are well formulated and communicated.
- Appropriate measures leads to attainment of strategic goals and impact the goals and strategies needed to achieve them.
- Performance measures should strongly align with the principal factors that determine competitive success and the strategic challenges the community faces.
- Performance measures should also be aligned with the BOD <u>leading</u> strategies and Management Company's <u>managing</u> action plans.

## Measuring reveals overall context and critical details to support the HOA today for the growth of tomorrow.
### Remember – everything is measurable!

**Measuring will**
- Track Trends
- Study Historical Data
- Analyze Strategies and Implementation
- Forecast Future Usage
- Address Issues
  Such as, how change is affecting the homeowners, which product/service is having the greatest improvement, and what aspects of product/service are generating inquiries both negative and positive.

**Performance Measurement will**
- Identify productivity and effectiveness of any function that can be measured by cost, time, quality, quantity or human relation.
- Promote productivity by focusing attention on issues important to the HOA.
- Look at both individual and group performance.
- Analyze effectiveness NOT efficiency.
- Motivate staff and make them feel better about what they are doing and themselves.

## You begin by reviewing costs, processes and reports that address your measurement goals and use the correct measurement tools!

## Step 1: Identify the Measurement Performance Goal(s)

Measuring should reflect the performance goal(s) and/or accomplishment(s) that your HOA wishes to address. Another words, if the goal is to measure *customer service* to homeowners, you may want to look at measures that reflect the incidence of complaints, response time, and survey results, to name a few.

# Examples of Some Measurement Goals

| Measurement Goal | Some Factors to Analyze |
|---|---|
| Recruitment | Cost per hire, source cost per hire, interviewing cost. |
| Selection | Time to fill position, time to start, job posting response rate-response factor-hire rate, and quality of hire. |
| Compensation and Benefits | Job posting factor, job evaluation factor, cost per compensation action, ratio of Human Resources staff to employee population, cost to supervise, pay and benefits as a % of total operating costs. |
| Record Keeping | Transaction processing rate cycle time and error rate, cost per transaction. |
| Performance Management | Meets by default rate, absence rate, absenteeism costs, effect of absenteeism of Labor Utilization, accession rate and separation rate. |
| Employee-Relations | Workforce stability and workforce instability factors, turnover/performance relationships, turnover costs, incidence of complaints or grievances by group, orientation costs per employee, employee satisfaction –suggestions and recognition rate. |
| Training and Development | Cost per trainee, training expenditures as a % of personal service expenditures, training development plan factor, skill change resulting from training, impact and value evaluation of training. |

## Step 2: Review Data

Once the HOA or management company identifies what it wants to measure than the collection and review of the applicable data begins.

*Review*

1. **Direct Costs** (Expenses and Savings)
   A. That are attached to a product or service
   B. That are tracked by an accounting system
   C. That are known and/or identified sometimes as overhead (overhead includes costs related to utility usage, and fixed cost that the employees use to do their job)

2. **Intelligent Analysis** (Analyzing processes –what happened, and why, when, where)
   A. Multiple data sources (manual files, computer files, past & present history)

B. Sophisticated reporting (reports, progress reports, financial reports)
C. In-depth knowledge (input from executives, staff, vendors)

3. **Straight Reporting** (Review reports to tell what happened)
   A. Single data source (employee performance logs, attendance reports)
   B. Top-level data points (Number of work orders, emails, telephone calls)
   C. Simple counts (orders to a particular vendor, complaints about an employee)

## Step 3: Calculate Performance

Although the HOA Board Members do not directly calculate performance of employees and projects they should understand and be able to evaluate the process the management company is using. This will assure that the HOA is receiving the best, cost effective and timely service available.

Of course many formulas exist to measure performance goals, and this booklet cannot discuss all of them; therefore, we selected a few that address some basic goals of an HOA.

### Cost per Hire

**Formula:** $CPH = \dfrac{Ad + AF + ER + T + Relo + RC \times 1.10}{H}$

| | |
|---|---|
| Ad = Advertising Fees | Relo = Relocation |
| AF = Agency Fees | RC = Recruiter Costs |
| ER = Employee Referrals | H = Number of Hires |
| T = Travel | 10% = All other overhead |

### Interviewing Costs

**Formula:** $C/I = \dfrac{ST + MT}{I}$

| | |
|---|---|
| C/I = Cost of Interviewing | ST = Staff Time Costs |
| MT = Management Time Costs | I = Number Interviewed |

# Quality of Hire

Formula: $QH = \dfrac{PR + HP + HS*}{N}$

*Additional indicators specific to your organization can be added here to customize the measure.

| QH = Quality of Hire | HP = % of new hires promoted within X period of time |
|---|---|
| PR = Average job performance rating of new hires | HS = number of indicators used |

# Employee Suggestions for Improvement

Formula: $ES = \dfrac{TS}{E/100}$     $SS = \dfrac{TSS}{TS}$

| ES = Employee suggestions per 100 employees | TS = Total number suggestions | E/100 = Total number of employees divided by 100 |
|---|---|---|
| SS = Savings per suggestions | TSS = Total savings resulting from suggestions | |

# Performance of a Project - Earned Value Analysis

According to the Project Management Body of Knowledge, **earned value analysis** is an objective method to measure project performance in terms of the triple constraints of scope, time and cost. This measuring technique is an excellent tool in assessing the health and applying metrics to the management of your project. Although I did not invent the "wheel" I certainly "re-configured it here" to make it more understandable.

*Project Example:* An HOA is doing some repairs to the swimming pool. The project is scheduled to take four-weeks and is budgeted at $10,000. The project manager, board or community manager at the third week meeting determined that the team has only completed 50% of the project. According to the project schedule the team was supposed to have completed 75% of the project at this point, AND it was discovered that $9,000 of the budget has been spent up to that date.

*What is the overall health of the project?*

**Measuring Projects Health:**

**Planned Value (PV)** represents the budgeted cost of all the planned tasks.
PV = Planned % Completed * Project Budget

**Earned Value (EV)** determines the amount of value that has been delivered to the project to date.  EV = Actual % Completed * Project Budget

**Actual Costs (AC)** determines the actual amount spent to a point against the project budget.
    **Example:**
    Planned Value 75%*$10,000 = $7,500
    Earned Value 50%*$10,000 = $5,000
    Actual Cost    $9,000

## Measuring Variances:

*Note: Variances should be **zero or greater**. Positive variances indicate a cost savings or schedule efficiency. Negative variances indicate deficiencies.*

**Cost Variance (CV)** determines the cost and schedule variances. Thereby measuring the actual costs of work performed to the project budget. CV=EV-AC

**Schedule Variance (SV)** determines the actual progress to the project schedule. SV=EV-PV
    **Example:**
    Cost Variance    $5,000-$9,000= ($4,000) negative
    Schedule Variance    $5,000-$7,500= ($2,500) negative

## Performance Index:

*Note: The index should be as close to 1 or greater. If the number is equal to 1 the project is on schedule. If they are greater than 1 then the project is ahead of schedule.*

**Cost Performance Index (CPI)** measures the project's earned value compared to the actual costs incurred. CPI=EV/AC

**Schedule Performance Index (SPI)** measures the actual progress to the project's schedule. SPI=EV/PV
    **Example:**
    Cost Performance Index    $5,000/$9,000 = .55 less than 1 – needs examined
    Schedule Performance Index $5,000/$7,500 = .66 less than 1 – needs examined

## Estimate of Completion:

**Estimate of Completion (EAC)** calculates the COST of the project if it continues on this path. It calculates the original budgeted actual costs (BAC) by the cost performance index. EAC=BAC/CPI
**Estimate of Completion –Example:**
    $10,000/.55 = $18,181
**Estimated Time to Completion (ETC) –Example:**
    1/.66*3 = 4.6 Weeks
ETC=1/SPI*Time (weeks/months at that point in time)

> **Example:**
> **If the project continues at this rate the project will cost the HOA $18,181 instead of the budgeted $10,000.**
>
> **AND it will take 4.6 weeks instead of the 4 weeks originally scheduled.**

Performance measurements is not an end in itself. It is only when someone uses these measures in some way do they accomplish something. Therefore, once the outcomes are analyzed, lessons are learned and applied, the HOA Board and Community Manager can begin to understand how well they are doing at accomplishing their goals. Now they need to inform the homeowners by **reporting and communicating the outcomes!**

"The good news is, homeowners are actually reading our association newsletter. The bad news is, they are starting to ask questions."

## LESSON 5: Communicating Outcomes

Once the measurements of performance have been completed the HOA Board needs to address areas that need improvement. Excellent, effective and productive communication is vital to the success of any organization; however within the HOA community homeowners expect immediate information. Therefore, the communication should not only be immediate, but needs to be designed in an easy format so not to raise questions among the homeowners. By planning what is said, how it is delivered and seeking feedback on how the message/information was received, a business professional ensures successful communication. Communication in business can be delivered verbally, non-verbally and written.

1. Adults place greater reliance on non-verbal clues than verbal clues in determining meaning.
2. That 60% to 65% of the meaning in a communication exchange is conveyed non-verbally.
3. Young children place great reliance on verbal cues (the words).
4. Reliance on non-verbal clues is greatest when there is a conflict between the verbal and non-verbal channels.
5. Non-verbal content is more important for judging emotional and attitudinal expressions, relational communication, and impression formation.

# Verbal Communication

Business professionals demonstrate effective verbal communication skills by conveying a verbal message clearly and concisely, acknowledging what the audience needs and speaking and using terminology the receiver understands. After all if the receiver does not correctly interpret the message than the communication was un-successful. Verbal communication in the HOA Community and within the Management Company occurs in many ways:

- **Meetings** where participants share their ideas, brainstorm, approve plans, communicate a change or get a status report.
- **Presentations** to convey their expertise on a particular topic, provide instruction, describe a product, policy or procedure. The presenter needs to keep the message clear by preparing adequately, use vivid language, use short words and sentences and allow time for the audience to ask questions and provide comments.
- **Conversations** can be both face-to-face and on the telephone and usually involve two or more people discussing a topic. For verbal conversations to be successful the speaker should be sensitive to the subject, time constraints and type of questions the receiver might ask.

# Non-Verbal Communication

Non-Verbal behaviors communicate intentional or non-intentional messages. This interpersonal communication is much more than the explicit meaning of words, the information or message intended. Non-Verbal communication includes facial expressions, gestures displayed through body language (kinesics), physical distance between the communicator (proxemics) and the tone and pitch of the voice. Some examples you may witness at the annual meeting:

- **Nodding of the head** colleagues may mean something very different from when the same action is used to acknowledge someone across a crowded room.
- **Signaling to others** that they have finished speaking or wish to say something.
- **Posturing** or how one sits or stands, whether their arms are crossed portrays a message.

# Written Communication

The important written forms of communication from the HOA and Management Company are the ones used to deliver information and for decision making, such as emails, newsletters, reports and diagrams to illustrate outcomes. Written documents can take the form of legal documents, for example, the governing documents. The written governing documents, policies and procedures ensure clarity among homeowners, employees and visitors, and minimize the chance for any misunderstanding.

- **Emails/Internet** is an extremely important tool used in business. Information delivered through emails can include setting up meetings, meeting agendas, and the status reports of projects. One needs to master the etiquettes required in constructing an email.

    **3 Step Process for Successful Emails**

    1. **Planning E-Mail messages**
    A. Pay attention to the email etiquette
    B. Make sure email is necessary
    C. Homeowners should follow the organizational hierarchy when sending a complaint – don't go straight to the board – give the management company the opportunity to address the issue.

    2. **Writing E-Mail Messages**
    A. DO NOT make readers have to decipher the meaning of your emails due to grammar errors, confusing sentences and miss-spelled words.
    B. Send perfect works of literature when emailing. Use effective subject lines.
    C. Keep emotions under control.
    D. Be aware that what you write in an email message could become public knowledge.

    3. **Completing E-Mail Messages**
    A. Revise and proof –careless writing is un-acceptable
    B. Verify before you hit SEND!

- **Internet/Disintermediation** as mentioned on page 18 and here again, Communication travels rapidly within the organization/community, because of the internet, email and technology. The internet has flattened the hierarchical diagram (Disintermediation) and has allowed employees/homeowners to send emails thereby sharing information and their opinions before leaders/board of directors have the opportunity to explain or fully justify their actions. However, the Internet has provided positive usage through e-Commerce and the ability to have websites. Websites enable the HOA through the Management Company websites and software to keep our community informed, updated and connected.

- **Newsletters** are a cost-effective medium for building relationships and maintaining regular contact with homeowners. Publishing a newsletter gives you the opportunity to increase awareness and understanding of the association, community and company services. Linking a newsletter to an informative website will provide a broader picture to your homeowners.

- The Content Marketing Institute found that 78% of respondents used newsletters.
- Nielsen Norman Group asked respondents how they preferred to receive company updates, and 90 % cited newsletters, compared to 10% for social media.

- **Reports** keep the business running smoothly, and saves the association time and money. Business reports, such as written business proposals are documents that describe the progress of the community and provides a means of comparing periods of time, project details and history of growth. Reports address all possible issues and questions for without reports no paper trails, nor budgets would exist, which both are vital for financial operation.

**Guidelines for writing the Business Proposal Are included in Appendix E**

**Financial EXCEL documents include:**
- Balance Sheet – illustrates account balances
- Income Statement – reports funds received
- Statement of Receivables – money due to HOA, collection and credits
- Bank Statements and Bank Reconciliation
- General Ledger – shows account activities

- **Diagrams** although many diagrams exist today to illustrate the performance and report the outcomes we are still seeing the "old school" charts being used. Therefore, in this lesson we are presenting the seven most common management and planning tools of today. Each diagram should be accompanied by a detailed report on the findings, problems, recommendations, solutions and changes the performance measurements indicated. Reporting the measurement indicators will help the HOA Board understand how well the HOA and Management Company is doing at accomplishing the goals and servicing the homeowners.

## 7 Management and Planning Tools

1. **Affinity diagrams**--great tool for a large association when organizing a large number of ideas, opinions, and facts relating to a broad problem or subject area within the community.

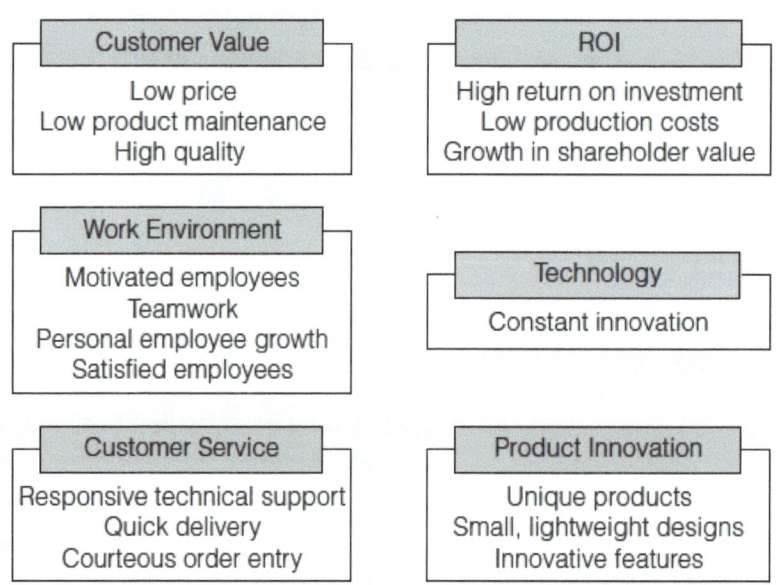

2. **Interrelationship digraphs**—will assist the HOA in identifying and exploring the many homeowner relationships among related ideas. It shows that every idea can be logically linked with more than one idea at a time, and allows for "lateral thinking" rather than "linear thinking."

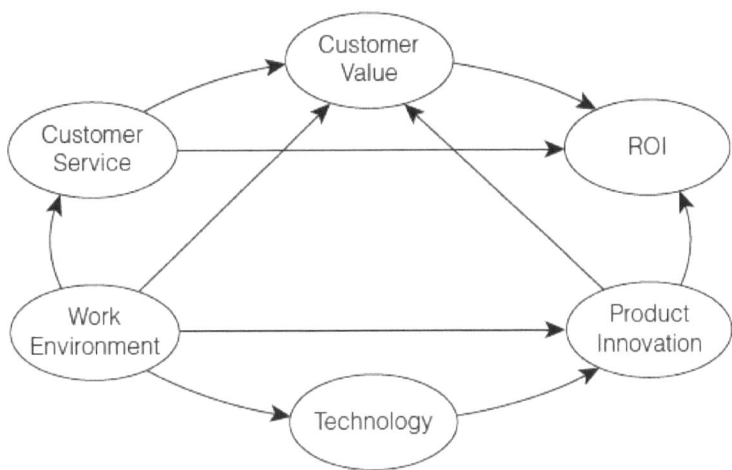

3. **Tree diagram**--Maps out the paths and tasks necessary to complete a specific project within the association/community or reach a specified goal.

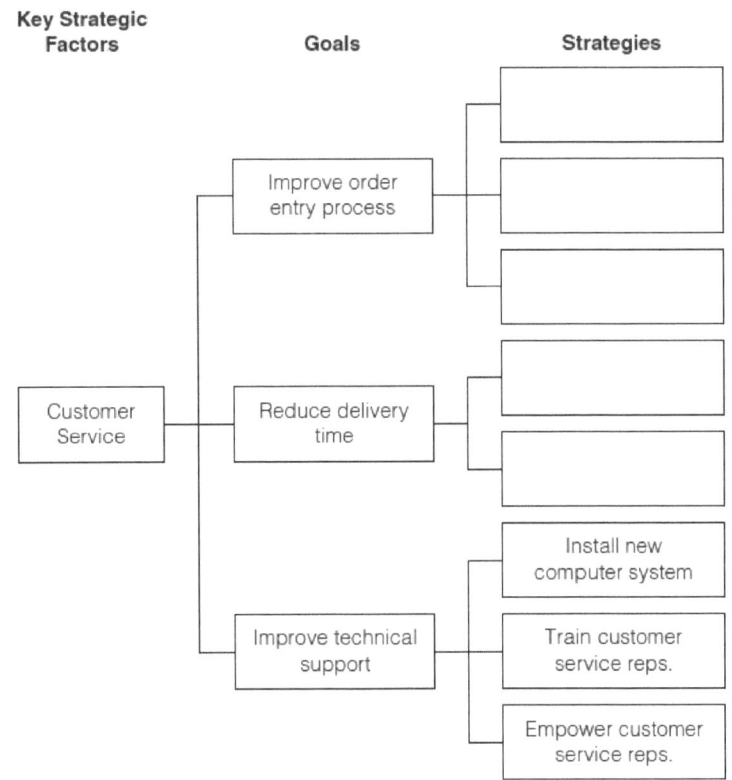

4. **Matrix diagrams**-- graphically display relationships between ideas, activities, or other dimensions in such a way as to provide logical connecting points between each item.

| Actions / Goals | Improve Work Environment | Improve Manufacturing Technology | Develop New Products |
|---|---|---|---|
| Cost Effectiveness | ● | ○ | |
| High Quality | ● | ● | |
| Shareholder Value | | △ | ● |

● = Strong relationship
○ = Medium relationship
△ = Weak relationship

5. **Matrix data analysis**--Takes data and arranges it to display quantitative relationships among variables to make them more easily understood and analyzed.

| Requirement | Importance Weight | Best Competitor Evaluation | MicroTech Evaluation | Difference |
|---|---|---|---|---|
| Price | .2 | 6 | 8 | +2 |
| Reliability | .4 | 7 | 8 | +1 |
| Delivery | .1 | 8 | 5 | −3 |
| Technical support | .3 | 7 | 5 | −2 |

6. **Process decision program chart**--A method for mapping out every conceivable event and contingency that can occur when moving from a problem statement to possible solutions.

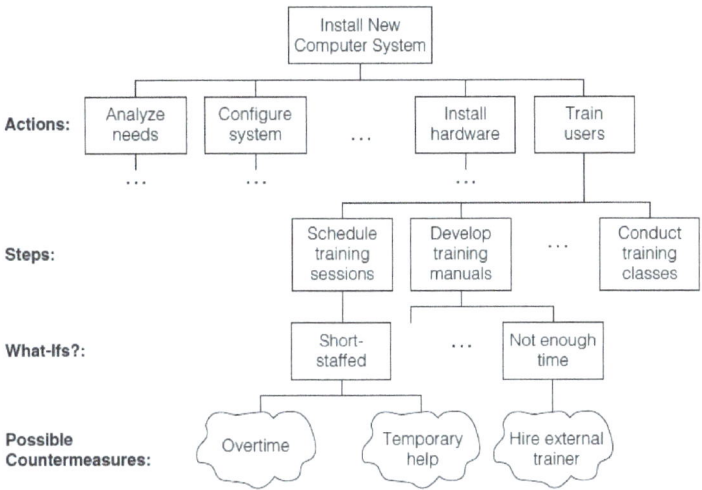

7. **Arrow diagrams**-- Arrow diagrams are another name for PERT/CPM project planning diagrams. This is often seen in computer and/or operations management with the term *network diagrams* for project planning and scheduling.

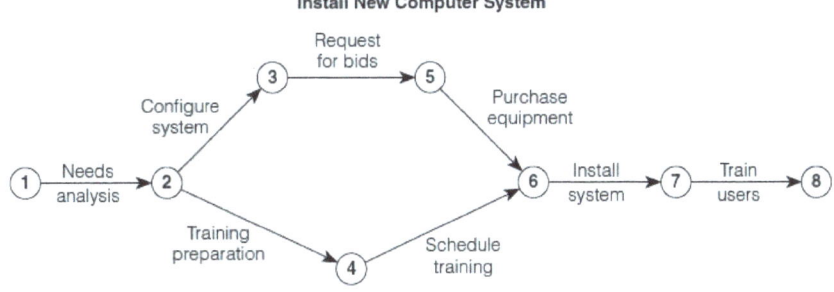

> **Cameron's Communication Plan can be found in Appendix F**

35

# Future Topics

**Book THREE will cover Pet Policies and the ADA among other topics.**

"Finally, the first approved pet for homeowner associations."

**Please email CameronSeminars@gmail.com with any topic ideas you have for future books. If the topic is selected, and upon your approval I will give credit to you in the book the topic is discussed.**

## References:

Cameron, Catherine A. Ph.D. (2009). Transitional Change Model

Cameron, Catherine A. Ph.D. 777 Business Program: ISBN-13: 978-1619274112.

Cameron, Catherine A. Ph.D. Business + Technology = Success: eBook www.amazon.com

Cherry, Kendra (2016). The Authoritarian Leadership Style & Others You Should Know. www.verywell.com/leadership-styles-2795312.

Cherry, Kendra (2016). The Major Leadership Theories, the Eight Major Theories of Leadership. www.verywell.com/leadership-theories-2795323.

Daft, Richard L. The Leadership Experience. 6th Ed. Cengage Learning

Evans, James R. & Lindsay, William M. (2013). Managing for Quality and Performance Excellence. Ninth Edition. Cengage Publishing.

Fitz-enz, Jac. (1995). How to Measure Human Resources Management. 2nd Ed. McGraw-Hill.

Gross, Debra; Akaiwa, Frank & Nordquist, Karleen (2014, 2011). Succeeding in Business with Microsoft Excel 2013 a Problem-Solving Approach. Cengage Publishing.

Kotter, John (1990). A Force of Change. Free Press

Lake, Rebecca (2015). Listening Statistics: 23 Facts You Need to Hear. www.creditdonkey.com/listening-statistics.html.

National Academy of Public Administration. (1997). Measuring Results: Successful Human Resources Management.

Phillips, Jack. (1996). Accountability in Human Resource Management.

Pinto, Jeffrey K. (2016). Project Management Achieving Competitive Advantage. Fourth Edition. Pearson Publishing.

www.businessballs.com

# APPENDIX A: Article
## ARE YOU CONFUSING LEADERSHIP AND CONTROL?
*4 Ways You Can Become a Person of Influence*
https://michaelhyatt.com/leadership-control-vs-influence.html

I often hear leaders, particularly younger ones, complaining about their lack of control in various situations. "If only the sales department reported to me, I could consistently hit my budget," they lament. Or, "If the production department reported to me, I would not have run out of inventory!"
What they are really saying is, "If I could control these people, I could guarantee the results."

Leadership is about influence, not control. I am not the first person to make this observation, but it is worth repeating. The truth is that *control is an illusion*. You can't control anyone, even the people that report to you. However, while you can't control anyone (except perhaps yourself), you can influence nearly everyone. This is the essence of true leadership.

By this definition, Jesus, Gandhi, and Martin Luther King Jr. were great leaders. They had control of virtually no one, yet their influence changed the course of history. Aspiring leaders would do well to stop focusing on control and figure out how to expand their influence. Here are four ways you can become a person of influence, no matter your position in your organization:

1. Focus on yourself. "If we could change ourselves," Gandhi said, "the tendencies in the world would also change. As a man changes his own nature, so does the attitude of the world change towards him?" Or as Saint Seraphim of Sarov said, "Save yourself, and you will save a thousand around you."
   Modeling is the most powerful form of teaching known to man. If you aren't "walking your talk," you dramatically lessen your influence. People have a hard time following leaders who say one thing and do another.
2. Take the initiative. Whiners are passive. They sit back and complain. They focus on what others should have done rather than what they themselves could have done. Real leaders don't have time to play the blame-game. Instead, they look for opportunities to take initiative and take action. There is always something you could be doing to influence the outcome.
3. Cast the vision. Oftentimes people don't do what we want, because we have not invested the time to paint the vision.
   In my experience, people want a challenge. They want to do something significant. They are eager to help. But no one has given them a compelling vision of a new reality. If you consider yourself a leader, this is your job.
4. Appreciate the effort. At the end of the day, everyone is a volunteer. Yes, even the people who report to you. They have more options than you think. If you don't appreciate them, someone else will.
   People want to give their best effort to those who notice. Time and time again, I have witnessed the power of a simple "thank you." If this is true for those who report to you, it is even truer of those who don't.

You can't control anyone, but you can influence nearly everyone. MICHAEL HYATT

# APPENDIX B: Exercise on Ethics

**Scenario**

As Asst. Community manager, you are responsible for monitoring the e-mail and Internet usage of the four people you supervise. If you find anything that violates the company's acceptable use policy, you are to report it to the Community manager.

Mary is not only your coworker, but she is also a good friend outside of work. Recently you found that Mary has been spending a large part of her workday researching health care and visiting the websites of assisted living centers. You know that Mary's father has been having some health problems. Mary is very concerned about her father and how best to handle his health care issues. But as Mary's supervisor you are concerned because much of her work day is being spent on personal issues. Her work is beginning to suffer.

**Discussion Questions**

1. What are the major ethical issues involved in this situation? _____
   _____
   _____

2. Would you talk to Mary as a friend? Why or why not? _____
   _____
   _____

3. Would you talk to Mary as her supervisor? Why or why not? _____
   _____
   _____

4. Would you report Mary's inappropriate use of company time to the department manager? Why or why not? _____
   _____
   _____

5. Would you ignore this and hope Mary corrects her work habits? Why or why not? ___
   _____
   _____

6. What do you think is the best approach to take to handle this situation?
   _____
   _____
   _____

# APPENDIX C: Listening Exercises

## LONDON BRIDGE Listening Exercise (Read out loud)
*Source: Section 1, 2 and 3 from* [www.Businessballs.com](www.Businessballs.com)

### Section 1

The first London Bridge was built by Romans sometime after AD43 and some of its wooden remains have been uncovered on the north side of the river. During its life the wooden structure was renewed several times, and it was probably to this earliest bridge that the nursery rhyme 'London Bridge is falling down' refers. Indeed, at one time, one of these structures was washed away by a flood, and another was torn down by invading Vikings, led by Olaf the Norseman in 1014.

The wooden structure was eventually replaced with a stone bridge, which commenced building in 1176 and featured twenty arches and stone piers with a drawbridge. This took thirty years to complete and houses and shops were incorporated to help pay for the upkeep of the bridge.

It would have been this bridge that was in place during Charles Dickens' youth and he remembered it in Great Expectations, when Pip crossed it in great despair, having recently learned that Estella was to be married to Drumlin. It also featured in his book David Copperfield, who spoke fondly of sitting in one of the stone recesses of the bridge, watching the people go by, or looking at the sun shining in the water and lighting up the golden flame on top of the Monument. One of these stone recesses has been preserved in the grounds of Guy's Hospital.

**Can you ANSWER the following questions without RE-READING?**

### Section 1 –

**What was the original structure of the bridge?**


**Who was Estelle going to marry?**


**What Nursery Rhyme was written after this bridge?**

_____

## Section 2

In 1825 a new bridge designed by John Rennie was opened, as the old one would no longer cope with the increasing traffic. This bridge was widened in 1902, and this bridge was featured in Dickens' book Oliver Twist. In fact the steps that used to lead down to the river to the west of the bridge were known as Nancy's Steps. This was due to the fateful conversation overheard by Noah Claypool between Nancy and Mr. Brownlow on a flight of steps on the Surrey bank, on the same side of the bridge as St. Savior's Church, which is now Southward Cathedral. Dickens' knowledge of this bridge enabled him to explain that Noah Claypool could conceal himself, yet still hear what was being said.

**Can you ANSWER the following questions without RE-READING?**

## Section 2 –

**Why was a new bridge opened in 1825?**

**What did Southwark Cathedral used to be called?**

**What book was the bridge featured in?**

_____

## Section 3

The stairs that are part of the bridge consist of three flights. Just below the end of the second, going down, the stone wall on the left terminates in an ornamental pilaster facing towards the Thames. At this point the lower steps widen so that a person turning the angle of the wall is necessarily unseen by any others on the stairs who chance to be above him, if only a step. It was in this way that Claypool was able to overhear the conversation which eventually leads to the death of Nancy at the hands of Bill Sykes.

In 1970, this bridge was sold to Lake Havasu City, Arizona, because a larger bridge was needed, and the bridge that we see today was finally opened in 1973. It is sometimes suggested by mischievous folk that the Americans thought they were buying the far more dramatic Tower Bridge, but no proof of this notion has ever been found.

**Can you ANSWER the following questions without RE-READING?**

## Section 3 –

**When was the bridge sold to Lake Havasu City?**


**Who overheard the conversation?**


**Who killed Nancy?**

_____

# LISTENING BEHAVIORS SURVEY
*Source: Dr. Cameron www.cameronseminars.com*

After each statement CHECK √ the block that best describes your behavior. After you complete this survey the interpretations are on the next page.

| STATEMENT | ALWAYS TRUE OF ME | SOMETIMES TRUE OF ME | NEVER TRUE OF ME |
|---|---|---|---|
| 1. I stay awake during work/meetings. | | | |
| 2. I maintain eye contact with speaker. | | | |
| 3. I don't pretend to be interested in topic. | | | |
| 4. I understand speaker's questions. | | | |
| 5. I try to summarize the information. | | | |
| 6. I look for organizational patterns (e.g. causes and effects, listing of items, etc.) | | | |
| 7. I set a purpose for listening. | | | |
| 8. I forego the temptation to daydream. | | | |
| 9. I try to predict what will come next. | | | |
| 10. I take notes regularly. | | | |
| 11. I ignore external distractions, such as loud noises, late arriving, etc. | | | |
| 12. I try to determine the speaker's purpose. | | | |
| 13. I recognize that the speaker may be biased about the topic. | | | |
| 14. I write down questions the speaker poses. | | | |
| 15. I copy down notes from the meeting. | | | |

Total the Yes's per column =   _____   _____   _____

# ANALYSIS OF RESULTS
## For the
## LISTENING BEHAVIORS SURVEY

**We are analyzing the number of YES's in the ALWAYS TRUE OF ME column and the NEVER TRUE OF ME column.**

## ALWAYS TRUE OF ME

14-15     you are a fantastic listener, both in a work or meeting setting and among your friends. Keep up the good work!

12-13     you are a good listener, however, you need to fine tune a few of your listening skills. Chose behaviors to modify that you feel will easily improve your listening and work or meeting performance.

10-11     you need to change behaviors so that you will get more out of work or meeting lectures. To improve your listening behaviors, you should start with any item that you marked as NEVER TRUE then move to the SOMETIMES TRUE column.

## 9 or more ALWAYS TRUE OF ME
## AND 7 or more NEVER TRUE OF ME

       At this point in your career path, you need to master listening skills for success. It will be difficult to find a situation in which you will NOT need to use listening skills.

# BARRIERS TO EFFECTIVE LISTENING

**Sometimes we set up barriers within ourselves to counteract good listening habits.**

*Source: Dr. Cameron www.cameronseminars.com*

The following survey will help you identify if you have any barriers to listening. CHECK the column that best answers the statement.

| Statement | YES | NO | Does not pertain to this lecture |
|---|---|---|---|
| 1. I usually think of this meeting or presentation as boring. | | | |
| 2. I pretend to be paying attention. | | | |
| 3. I don't like the speaker's mannerisms (e.g., pacing, phrasing). | | | |
| 4. I tried to take notes on "everything" which was said during the meeting. | | | |
| 5. I tried to write my notes in complete sentences. | | | |
| 6. The subject for this meeting was way too difficult for me. | | | |
| 7. Some personal problems kept my mind busy during the meeting or presentation. | | | |
| 8. I didn't waste my time in writing down information from the PowerPoints or video. | | | |
| 9. I was really angry about something the speaker said during the meeting or presentation. | | | |
| 10. I definitely enjoyed distractions more than the meeting or presentation (e.g. people arriving late) | | | |
| 11. I spent much of the meeting or presentation with a good daydream. | | | |
| 12. I didn't' really understand the meeting or presentation, but did not ask questions. | | | |

**YES answers** **mean barriers exist and indicate you need to change to become a better listener.** *You should take this survey after other meetings to identify if your barriers are being eliminated.*

**NO answers** **mean NO BARRIERS EXIST**

# APPENDIX D: Cameron's Change Model

# CAMERON's CLUE©

Although most change is still a hierarchical process when it comes to policy making, it is the communication and philosophy of how to introduce CHANGE, which has changed. Today communication travels rapidly within the organization/community, because of the internet, email and technology. The internet has flattened the hierarchical diagram and has allowed employees/homeowners to send emails thereby sharing information and their opinions before leaders/board of directors have the opportunity to explain or fully justify their actions. Therefore, the change agents have to be aware of this instantaneous delivery, and although they cannot control it, they can prepare for it. Leaders/HOA Boards today must include their employees/homeowners in the decision making process, which can be done by forming committees. Committees permit the stakeholders to have input into change or addressing issues and this will greatly decrease the negative discussions about the change and increase the positive input.

## Cameron's Formula for Implementing Change
### G + O + A + L + S = Successful Change©

| | |
|---|---|
| **G** | From the beginning the **GOALS** and need for the change must be discussed, planned, and communicated to all stakeholders that it will affect. Organize a committee that is charged with developing the change process. The committee will develop and administer a survey that will be distributed to the entire organization/community. This will keep all stakeholders informed and get their input on the change process. |
| **O** | The change must be **OBTAINABLE and ORGANIZED**. The change must be needed and be an obtainable change. The change must be realistic. If it is not realistic it will not be accepted and therefore, implementation will not be successful. Also the change process should be presented in an organized, well designed and communicated process to not only those affected, but to the entire organization/community. Explain the "why, when and how" the change will be taking place. The more details the better. (***The Road to Success is Paved with Details***. A poster designed by William D. Cameron found on the website www.cameronseminars.com) |
| **A** | There should be an **AWARD** to those that embrace the change. Awards can be verbal recognition, a gift or luncheon. It should be a company/community-wide announcement and be well communicated. This will foster future cooperation in implementing change within your organization/community. |
| **L** | After the change is implemented make sure you **LISTEN** to your employees/homeowners. Address resistance to the change by again reminding the stakeholders of the "why" change was necessary. Also make sure supervisors/board members are addressing any negative talk happening within the company/community, and do not ignore it. |
| **S** | **SHARE** feedback. Make sure the successes and failures of the change implementation are noted, recorded and discussed. This will ensure future successful change! |

# APPENDIX E: Writing the Business Proposal

## Writing the Business Proposal

*Pointers:*
- *Organize the contents of the Proposal*
- *Write in a professional manner*
- *Keep your audience in mind and write to their level*

| Description | Suggestion |
|---|---|
| Cover Letter | List the people who did the study, summarize objectives, it can also note the time and place of any oral presentations. |
| Title Page | Name of the project, the names of the systems analyst, team members, date the proposal is submitted. Titling is more of an art than a science. Keep page uncluttered and presentable. |
| Table of Contents | Not necessary if proposal is less than 10 pages. Use subheadings to help reader find the information easier. |
| Executive Summary | Is critical and highly used in the business world today. Should be 250-375 words that provide the … who, what, when, where, why and how of the proposal. |
| Outline of Proposal/Study | Information about all the methods used in the study and who or what was studied. Questionnaires, surveys, interview, sampling, observation notes –all should be discussed and if suggested included in the appendices. |
| Detailed Results | Report on the details that the systems analyst has found out about the system through all the methods discussed in the prior section. |
| Alternatives | Present two or three alternative solutions that directly address the problem. Each alternative should be explored and presented separately and state what management needs to do or not do in each alternative. |
| Recommendations | After weighing all the alternatives select the one that best solves the problem. Express the recommendation so that it is easy to understand and present it in a logical format. |
| Summary | Brief statement that mirrors the content of the executive summary. It should not quote the material from the executive summary verbatim. It gives the project's importance and feasibility along with the value of the recommendation. |
| Appendices | Any information you feel is of interest. Examples: summary of phases completed in the study, detailed graphs and documentation to support your findings. |

# APPENDIX F: Cameron's Communication Plan

## The Communication Plan©

### PURPOSE
Helps keep communication focused and assures that the company takes full advantage of all opportunities. It also identifies existing marketing and communication capabilities.

### WHEN DEVELOPING Build *before strategic planning begins*
- Create around time of change (start-up implementation, or change of existing procedure)
- Set up a tracking system (ex. journal, photographs).
- Develop a "look" or uniformed layout for all strategic planning documents and printed material.
- Incorporate two-way communication utilizing your local area network (ex. intranet, email).
- Segment the community into separate manageable parts.
- Organize a steering committee made up of volunteers.
- Use communication vehicles such as, meetings, community town meetings, and media releases.
- Include detailed information on beliefs, missions, etc. in newsletters or other media releases.

### COMMUNICATING CHANGE
1. Ask people for their opinion before you implement
2. Explain the change in language people understand.
3. Explain how the change will affect the people.
4. Anticipate how people will react.
5. Design your communication to answer those concerns.
6. Expect the change to generate resistance.
7. Encourage your people to participate in the implementation of the change.
8. Keep communicating about the change even after its implementation.
9. CELEBRATE its success.

### INTERNAL COMMUNICATION
Staff should be kept informed from the design phase all the way through to implementation. Ways to keep your staff informed may include some or all of the following:
- Staff newsletter, memo or flyers.
- Steering committee volunteers can inform and educate.
- Focus groups
- Department meetings
- Speakers and informative sessions

# THE COMMUNICATION PLAN©

1. Does your company have a uniformed "look" or layout for all internal marketing and communication material?
2. What written communication is available?

| Internal Written Communication | YES | NO | How often does this type of communication take place per year? | Comments: Likes, dislikes, efficient, inefficient, etc. WHY? |
|---|---|---|---|---|
| Memorandum | | | | |
| E-mail messages | | | | |
| Newsletters | | | | |
| Letters with the paychecks | | | | |
| Employee handbook or policy updates | | | | |
| Job satisfaction survey | | | | |
| Bulletin board or computer message board postings | | | | |
| Brochures | | | | |
| Other - Explain | | | | |

3. What verbal communication situations are taking place?

| Internal Verbal Communication | YES | NO | How often does this type of communication take place per year? | Comments: Likes, dislikes, efficient, inefficient, etc. WHY? |
|---|---|---|---|---|
| Plant meetings- Regional Meetings | | | | |
| Staff meetings – departmental | | | | |
| Feedback sessions | | | | |
| Teleconferences | | | | |
| Informal – hall, water cooler, etc. | | | | |

4. Does the Customer Service (CS) department (or person) view their role in the marketing or communication function as a delegate, the go to person, or does CS handle it all? WHY do you believe this to be the case?
5. How many staff members are responsible for marketing and communication? List their names and titles.

©Dr. Catherine A. Cameron, Cameron Seminars www.cameronseminars.com

**Dr. Cameron's Closing Comments:**
You can find my bio and books on my website www.cameronseminars.com. I hope you found this information helpful and it guides you on your road to success. Please email me any suggestions of future topics and as a special "thank you" email your request for a FREE copy of your choice of either…

**7 Cameron Clue's**
**Myers and Briggs Personality Test**
**DISC Factor Analysis**

***Learn what you need to SUCCEED!***
***Dr. Cathy Cameron***

Cameron Seminars and Consulting, LLC www.cameronseminars.com can bring a seminar to your HOA board or business.

---

**William D. Cameron, Co-Author:**

Bill has over 40 years of industry experience in facility and operations management. He held the position of Vice President of Operations for Point Park University in Pittsburgh, Pennsylvania where he provided leadership and direction to the departmental areas of Planning, Project Management, Physical Plant, Transportation, Event Planning, Mailroom/Receiving and Public Safety with approximately 100 direct or indirect reports. Bill retired in 2013 to his home in Myrtle Beach that he has owned with Cathy since 1995. Bill earned the reputation for achieving extreme productivity in meeting operations and production objectives, demonstrating exceptional skill when working under pressure, taking the initiative in judgment and decision making and ensuring compliance with all safety, quality and industry standards: all while working within the budget. His extensive training in specialized areas and education at the Institute of Real Estate Management (IREM) Certified Property Management Program provided input and direction in various areas of this training manual.

You can purchase William's **poster** found on the back cover.